SJS 266   N/3.00

P

THE RAWHIDE RAILROAD

BY GEORGE ESTES

Published by

George Estes' Publishers

Cedarwood,

Rte. 1, Troutdale, Oregon

——o——

Press of The Canby Herald

Canby, Oregon

FACSIMILE REPRODUCTION 1971
THE SHOREY BOOK STORE
815 Third Avenue
Seattle, Washington 98104

SECOND PRINTING
Of Facsimile Reprint

Limited to 200 Copies
October 1974

ISBN #0-8466-0266-0

DEDICATED

To

The Pioneer Railroad Builders
of the Pacific Northwest,

WHO, undaunted by dangers, undismayed by difficulties, builded their Hopes and Dreams into The Empire of the Columbia,

This book is affectionately dedicated by the author, whose parents toiled over the Old Oregon Trail by ox-team in eighteen hundred, fifty.

GEO. ESTES.

Cedarwood,
Rte. 1, Troutdale, Ore.—1924.

To Dad

from Mary + Mike

Christmas

1977

CONTENTS

ILLUSTRATIONS

THE RAWHIDE RAILROAD
HEADENDUM
Preface to first edition.

This is a story of a remarkable steam railroad actually constructed and successfully operated in the beautiful Walla Walla Valley many years ago, on which rawhide, overlaying wooden beams, was used in place of iron or steel rails. This unique road, later modernized, is now operated as part of a large railway. It is doubtful, however, if through the roll of years, the changing managements of the big line have preserved either record or recollection of the once famous rawhide railroad, which was the germ of the present transportation system.

More than a quarter century ago, while in railroad service, it was my good fortune to come in contact with an old Irish section foreman, long since dead, who had been actually employed on the singular railroad. The outlines of the narrative were extracted from him disjointedly and at different times, but the wealth of detail and circumstantial accuracy leaves no doubt of the truth of the story as a whole.

After the catastrophe, which closes the last chapter, the railroad was operated successfully for many years with iron plates fastened on top of the wooden rails. Then the road was purchased by the Oregon Railway and Navigation Company, and is now part of that great railroad system.

GEO. ESTES.

Cedarwood—1916.
Rte. 1, Troutdale. Or.

PREFACE TO SECOND EDITION

The attention of the world was directed to this booklet by a full page article in The Saturday Evening Post of May 6, 1922, which contained the following:

"It contains as much Homeric humor of the American West as anything between covers since the days of Mark Twain's 'Roughing It.'"

A second edition has become necessary and is now offered to the public with the information that Dorsey S. Baker, the "Doc Baker" of the story, was a living character of tremendous force and executive ability as the story shows.

Strangely the Baker family have taken exception to the story, calling it a burlesque.

The author thought his story redounded to the great honor of it's principal character.

He warns the public at this late date that the amusing incidents and humor of the story are from the author's brain.

But the peerless Walla Walla Valley,

The Mighty Columbia River,

The thousand cut-throats of Wish-ram,

Ladd's Bank, older than any other National Bank and

The successful building of the railroad by Doc Baker, the hero of the story, are great FACTS as lasting and imperishable as the far flung range of the Blue Mountains.

GEO. ESTES.

Cedarwood—1924.

Rte. 1, Troutdale, Or.

CHAPTER I.

WALLA WALLA

Because of the massacre of a missionary and all his family a frowning fort had been established, manned with soldiers and armed with cannon, in the center of a great empire of the richest land on earth.

In time a village grew up around the fort. They named it Walla Walla after the Injun's name for the valley empire in which the fort and village were located. The Injun's traditions told that in the beginning a wall of water extended high above the whole great valley and in after ages sawed a way out through the rim and poured down the deep gorge of the Columbia to the sea.

When the water gushed out through the break in the western wall, the undulating bottom land of fertile silt was laid bare. In this rich soil are embedded smooth cobblestones, rounded by the ceaseless roll of waters, which swept them back and forth on the bottom of the ancient sea for countless ages—silent but unimpeachable witnesses to the truth of the Injun legend.

An old Injun trail, still clearly traced, starts at the fort, marks its winding thread across the shallow depressions, creases the gentle slopes and deeply scars the low ridges and, stretching away to the northeast, leads to the gold-bearing country beyond Lewiston.

Far to the southeast hangs a long, dark, cloud of beautiful indigo, swinging low in the sky. It hung there just the same way before they built the village; even before the fort was constructed, and a thousand ages before the cruel massacre which caused its building. One end of the blue starts at the sunrise and the other end hangs over the western rim of the world.

That is the Blue Mountain range.

Its blue is different from any other blue. Its corrugated azure chain is linked through the center of the Wenaha National forest. It is the most striking feature of the great empire, over whose approach from the south and east it stands guard, even as the winding stream of Snake River protects the north, and the rolling waters of the mighty Columbia watch the west.

Under the shadow of the fort the village grew and the broad valley prospered. The long trails of the men who brought rich peltries and glistening gold led to the village out of the land of the sunrise, and from the Salmon River country and from the Seven Devils mines, which lay beyond the low cloud of indigo. The grizzled trappers and bearded miners traded the peltries and yellow pebbles and golden sands for flour, bacon and plug tobacco and for gold pans and quicksilver at the stores in the village.

The trails that led from the mines to the village were many and smoothly worn, and the gold dust that came over them weighed heavy in the buckskin bags. Because of this there was a

big trail that came to the village from the other way, from the great river that rolled along in the sunset down in the west—for there is always a broad road to the place where the bags of gold weigh heavy.

CHAPTER II.

THE RAILROAD BUILDER

Pioneer days in western lands breed strange people and produce remarkable characters. Society is unorganized and conditions are primitive. The law does not, for a time, acquire the steady control over men, which is necessary to prevent crimes against persons and property.

Such times and places develop strong personalities, many of whom are questionable, if not wholly bad. But almost invariably some one man climbs to the top and ultimately stands as far above the general run of the community as the rugged crown of Hood's mighty mountain towers above the western world.

In the broad empire of Walla Walla these times brought out their strong man. He was rough with that ruggedness that marks the man who stalks in the open in times of danger and knows that he can protect himself and his from enemies coming four ways at once. The only name ever given him by the hardy settlers was Doc Baker. His many friends loved him by that name. The disappointed sharpers, who had tried to bunco him and failed, hated him by the same name, but he commanded the respect of friends and enemies alike. Managed with rare judgment his goods multiplied. He acquired thousands of rolling acres of the rich silt land of the Walla Walla. His cattle fattened on the tall grasses growing in green profusion on a thousand hills.

In August his wheatfields waved goldenbronze in a thousand gentle valleys. He owned pasture lands, and timber lands, and orchard lands and meadow lands.

But this was by no means all the wealth of Doc Baker.

CHAPTER III.

THE PIONEER BANK

Far—and again far—down in the west toward the sunset, past the long stretches of treeless lands, around roaring rapids in the great river where sat the Injun village of Wish-ram, through a walled stone gorge, sawed down a mile through a mountain range—is a place where another great river, the Willamette, comes into the Columbia from the south. Here a small village had started, composed mostly of log cabins with the stumps still standing in the streets. They named it Portland because the two men who owned the place tossed up a coin (which they had brought with them around the Horn) and the man who came from Maine won twice in the toss-up against the man who came from Boston.

In this village there was one particular log cabin which people called a "Bank." It had been started by a young man a few years before, and his careful attention to the business had caused the little community to look upon his log cabin bank much the same as we now regard the United States Treasury. They were justly proud of the bank, because it was the only one between the Rocky Mountains and the sea, up and down the long coast line from the frozen fields of the polar bear to the sun-scorched shores of Panama, and it had been started before any National Bank in the United States came into existence. Its capital was twenty-five thousand dollars. Men knew what that meant because they had seen minted dollars before they left home on their journey into the sunset, around the Horn. Its interest rate was two per cent a month; a reasonable charge to men who could have paid ten times that and still have made money.

On the books of the bank was an account in the name of Doc Baker, which could have had many checks of five figures drawn against it and the account would still have contained five figures. And yet Doc Baker had never put in the bank a dollar of money bearing the imprint of the United States. His deposits had been composed of yellow "dust" from beyond the Blue Mountains and minted slugs of gold bearing the design of a beaver and the legend 5D or 10D, which passed for money in the Oregon Country. But the certificates given by Ladd's Bank for these deposits called for money of the United States and they were accepted by all men, then as now (half a century later), at their face in the Oregon Country, or for that matter in any other land where men had need of money.

CHAPTER IV.

THE COLUMBIA RIVER

The greatness of the Columbia River is but dimly realized. Including its tributaries, it is navigable for many thousand miles in the United States, and what can be said of no other river, for thousands of miles in foreign lands, before its clear waters wash our native soil. The gorge of the Columbia, which is the mile deep crevice it has cut for a roadway a hundred miles through the Cascade range, is one of the wonders of the world. The waterfalls of immense height and fantastic form, which leap over the towering escarpments and plunge downward to the river below as if dropped from the clouds, have no parallel in other lands.

At Wallula, the nearest point on the river to Walla Walla, one bright spring day a painted

cedar canoe, with high upturned prow, rested partly on the yellow sands of the shore and partly on the heaving surface of the river. It had been colored jet black with stain made from iron float and juice of the white oak apples and then striped in odd figures of Injun design, in red ochre mined from deep crevices in the mountains, and brilliant green made from the juice of the nettle stalk. Seated in the canoe, eating jerked venison, were two Klickitat Injuns, one tall and thin, the other short and pudgy. They were Doc Baker's boatmen, awaiting his arrival over the trail from Walla Walla, to

take him down the river to the village of Portland.

These two Injuns were odd characters. Their names were Sapolil and Seekolicks, which showed both the practical and sentimental side of the Injun. Sapolil being inclined to take on flesh was himself the logical reason for the name he bore. His full name was Marmora Sapolil, which means "Injun's bread," i. e., cakes made from the native plant of that name, which grows wild in great profusion on the Pacific Coast. Being a necessity of life, the practical nature of Sapolil's name is at once apparent.

Seekolicks had come by his title rather differently, showing the sentimental side of the Injun. His name in the Chinook tongue means "breeches." At that time breeches were merely a luxury among the Klickitats and in fact were considered too advanced to be in prevailing style along the Columbia. However, Seekolicks was generally looked upon as one of the best dressers that ever came down the river, and his resplendent breeches were the cause of many admiring glances from the coy maidens of Wish-ram, the village at the great rapids, and in very truth his raiment was of the gorgeous colors of the sunset, albeit he confined himself entirely to breeches, as the fashion of wearing shirts and other garments had not yet come in. It might be said that the breeches bore a peculiar resemblance to a red flannel shirt. In fact, it had been whispered up and down the river that Seekolicks had been so fortunate as to find an old red shirt, discarded by some opulent miner, and by inverting it had used the arms for legs, fastening the tail up around his waist with a thong of deer sinew. Thus clad, Solomon in all his glory had nothing on Seekolicks.

At this point the story teller, who writes by rule, will say that too much attention is being devoted to Seekolick's breeches. He will wag his head sententiously and remark that nothing should be put into the story that does not advance the plot according to the patented method of writing short stories. But our story is not being written according to the patent, but according to the facts and besides upon Seekolicks' pants hangs the fate of a great empire, as we shall see. But for the overwhelming desires and passions of the savage tribes, inflamed to the burning heat by these bright pants, the Rawhide Railroad might never have existed and the Pacific Northwest might yet remain a wilderness.

In time Doc Baker arrived at the river, mounted on his favorite mule and accompanied by two horsemen carrying heavy buckskin bags. The bags were carefully deposited in the bottom of the painted canoe and the two horsemen leading Doc Baker's mule galloped away over the trail back to Walla Walla.

The Injun boatmen shoved the canoe off shore and with Doc Baker seated in the center, shot swiftly down the swirling stream. The wonders of the mighty river rapidly sped by on either hand, but the solitary passenger in the graceful canoe scarcely heeded them, being engrossed in weighty plans for the future. Rapidly the miles of water lengthened behind them as they stopped only to cook and prepare food at favorable points along the shore and for a short period for rest and sleep. On the fourth day they arrived at the mouth of another large river, the Willamette, and, turning up this wide stream, the canoe soon plowed its nose into the sandy shore opposite the village of Portland.

SKOOKUM CHICKAMIN

BANK RULES

10 Coon Skins—1 Deer hide.

10 Deer Hides—1 Mink Peltry.

10 Mink Peltries—1 Beaver Pelt.

3 Beaver Pelts—1 oz. Gold Dust.

Skunk skins are not liquid assets and must not be brought into the bank.

Promissory notes must be written on buckskin.*

Customers drawing on each other in the bank must step outside before shooting.

This rule has got to be lived up to.

*In the early days of the Oregon country a promissory note written on buckskin was not affected by the statute of limitations and never ran out.

Here Doc Baker landed and beckoning the Injuns to follow with the buckskin bags, went up
the trail that led to Ladd's bank. They follow-
ed in single file and dumped their burden on the
bank's counter, composed of half a fir log with
the flat side up. As they deposited their heavy
load Sapolil muttered in gutteral tones something that sounded like "Skookum chickamin,"
which indicated that the wily Injun was assimi-
lating the ways of his white brother. He had
discovered the two things nearest the white
man's heart and person: money and breeches.
"Skookum chickamin" translated both literally
and freely means "Big money" and so the un-
lettered savage understood "Big money" and
was beginning to learn about breeches. It needed only firewater to complete his civilization.

The two bags weighed seventy-eight pounds
Troy, on the bank's scales. Doc Baker had not
come down the river to bring this stuff to the
bank. He brought it because it was in the way
at home, but his business was far weightier
than that. Mr. Ladd asked him to wait a minute
until he made the entry in his books "before he
forgot it," and then they would have a smoke

and talk things over. Mr. Ladd put down the number "15" with three ciphers to the right, in the credit column of the account of Doc Baker and they were then ready to smoke.

It was something really important that had brought Doc Baker down the long journey from Walla Walla to see Mr. Ladd.

Had Mr. Ladd ever heard of railroads?

Yes, he had heard of railroads.

What was a railroad like?

Mr. Ladd described a railroad.

Doc Baker concluded that he wanted a railroad from Walla Walla to the river, so that the golden grain of his thousand valleys could be conveyed to the great water-way.

Could Mr. Ladd get him two locomotives?

Yes, Mr. Ladd could send a letter to his banking correspondent in New York, around the Horn.

There was no other way. The distance to New York and back that way was near enough twenty thousand miles. The New York house, on the order of Mr. Ladd, would buy two locomotives, whatever their cost might be, ship them back around the Horn and bill the expense to the bank, which in turn would charge the account of Doc Baker. It was all so simple and easy. The letter would go to New York and the locomotives be shipped back and reach Portland in two years from that time, and they would then be started up the river for Wallula.

Mr. Ladd wanted to know what Doc Baker would do about the iron rails for his road?

Do? He would put down wooden rails, big and strong, and even if they did wear out fast they could be cheaply replaced.

Mr. Ladd's next question was as to a civil engineer to survey, construct and maintain the roadway, and a train dispatcher to move trains and conduct transportation.

Doc Baker was stumped for a few moments —but not long. He remembered that he had met and overcome every difficulty besetting him in life so far. He would provide a civil engineer who could survey and construct the roadway.

How long would it take to survey the road from Walla Walla to Wallula?

Mr. Ladd thought it would require about six months. Preliminary surveys must be run, levels must be ascertained, meander lines drafted, cross-sectioning completed, grade stakes set. This was all a little puzzling to Doc Baker, but the train dispatcher was more so. However, he had made up his mind to build and operate a railroad from Walla Walla to the river, and that point once settled, all else would follow.

His next question caused young Ladd to lose the grip on his clay pipe and it tumbled down and crashed to fragments on the split puncheon floor of the log cabin bank.

"Could any plug hats be had in Portland?"

This was so absurd that Mr. Ladd roared with laughter and then answered that the plug hat did not thrive west of the Missouri river, owing to the lack of demand and the manifest danger to the wearer on account of the irresistible impulse which would be sure to possess the first miner loaded with "yellow jacket juice" to shoot a hole through it.

However, Doc Baker told Mr. Ladd that he thought some plug hats might be needed in connection with the railroad.

And so it fell out that a letter was started by the first sailing vessel leaving Portland for New York, around the Horn, giving the New

York correspondent bank full power to purchase two narrow guage locomotives, one hundred pairs of car wheels and one thousand plug hats and ship them back to Ladd's bank.

CHAPTER V.

THE CHIEF ENGINEER

Doc Baker went back up the river in the painted canoe, paddled by the same two Injuns, Sapolil and Seekolicks.

He told the Injuns what he had done. They had great faith in him, but thought that maybe he and Mr. Ladd might have had too much firewater together. Sometimes the white man did that way, and when he did, he couldn't talk sense for a time. Possibly Doc Baker had done as others did. The two Injuns talked it over and shook their heads. They hoped that it might be that way and that the Devil's wagon that he had told them about, that ate up wood and shot smoke and fire out of its head was not a real thing but only fire-water talk, which the sagacious Injuns had long since discovered did not last.

As soon as Doc Baker arrived home he began planning the construction of the railroad. Mr. Ladd had said the first requisite was a chief engineer to survey the line and then to build and keep it up afterwards. Doc Baker debated this matter in his mind for some time and finally decided on Bill Green. Bill had many qualifications for the position. He could drive a thorough-brace stage coach, loaded with passengers and gold-dust and pulled by six horses, closer to the edge of a precipice, without going over, than any other man in the country. This showed ability to calculate distances accurately. With a Colt's revolver he had winged a horse-thief in full flight on a cayuse pony when he was just disappearing below a ridge, showing ability to sight straight, which Mr. Ladd said was a qualification required of a civil engineer. He could drive twenty yoke of oxen so that all would pull evenly on the load, showing generalship and the power to command. Mr. Ladd also said that a chief engineer should have some knowledge of law, on account of right-of-way disputes. Bill had once been foreman on an impromptu jury for a justice of the peace acting as coroner and had sat on the remains of a bully who had terrorized the country, but who had at last been killed by a quiet citizen with whom the bully had picked a quarrel—the quiet citizen having pulled quicker than the bully. The verdict of the jury voiced by Bill Green, was that the bully had died from contributory negligence, which gave great satisfaction to the community, and had at once proven Bill a man of tact as well as deeply learned in the law.

So resourceful a man could undoubtedly survey and build a railroad. He was therefore appointed chief engineer and notified that he was to employ as many men as required and obtain all the material needed, and proceed at once to survey and locate the road from Walla Walla to Wallula, and that the work of surveying must be entirely finished in six months, the time set by Mr. Ladd.

The first move of the chief engineer showed the man of tact. He had never seen a railroad, nor, for that matter, had he ever heard of a transit or a level. Books of logarithms and traverse tables were as uncommon to him as the binomial theorem to hungry wolves in the Blue Mountains.

Ground-sluicing in the Salmon River mines was an Irishman named Pat Prunty, who had given out that he was at one time a section foreman on an eastern railroad and was accordingly looked upon with some degree of wonder by those who had never seen a railroad. This man was sent for by Bill Green and when he arrived he was asked to tell all he knew about a railroad

The ex-section foreman explained about surveying and grading road-beds, and the use of the transit and levels, which of course could not be had in Walla Walla. But Bill Green, having learned what was required and that ten degree curves and two per cent grades should be the maximum, readily entered into the spirit of the work. He ascertained that ten degrees was a bend of ten inches from a straight line in sixty-six and six-tenths feet, that a two per cent grade was a rise of 105 feet in a mile. The rest was easy for this resourceful westerner.

Mounted on mules and accompanied by two assistants provided with axes, tape line and a whiskey flask half filled with water, to be used as a lock level by sighting across the surface of the water in the flask held horizontal, the road

THE CHIEF ENGINEER

was surveyed and the grade stakes set by these mule-back engineers, from terminus to terminus, in six days, instead of six months, to the intense satisfaction of Doc Baker. What is more, in after years when the road was successfully operated as a part of a great railway, no fault was found with the mule-back survey.

The work of grading proceeded with equal rapidity. Bill Green used twenty yoke of oxen—forty great animals of immense power, hitching them to a grader constructed by himself. On each side of the grader was a mule team hitched to a boom. The drivers of the mules kept the grader in position by pulling on it diagonally with the mule teams. There was an ox driver with a goad stick for every four yoke of oxen.

Mounted on his mule and carrying an enormous black-snake whip, the chief engineer galloped down the long line of oxen and started up the leaders first, to take up the slack in the drag chain, which was larger in size successively between each yoke from the front to the rear. Then galloping along the far-flung length of this tremendous team, the versatile chief engineer sent out a running fire of concussions from the blacksnake whip, which sounded like a battle of six-pounders, and the mighty team bent their necks to the yokes and the great steel blades of the grader, guided by the two mule teams, bit into the soft earth and traveled slowly but steadily from Walla Walla to Wallula and the grading was done and the roadbed ready for the ties.

Meantime many hewers on the mountains and in the quarries had been squaring stones and felling timbers which were brought to the graded roadway and worked into the culverts, and used for ties and wooden rails as planned by Doc Baker.

The ties were laid, and the heavy wooden stringers to take the place of iron rails were laid transversely upon them. Only the stringers on one side of the track were spiked down to the ties. Those on the other side could not be spiked because there was no way of telling what the gauge of the locomotives would be. There was no telegraph line and the mail could not travel any faster around Cape Horn than the locomotives themselves.

Everything was completed for the thirty miles between Walla Walla and Wallula except spiking the one rail.

CHAPTER VI.

THE INJUN MESSENGERS

Two years after the time when this story begins, the high-prowed canoe, covered with quaint red and green designs, glided smoothly on the long journey from Portland to Walla Walla. Sapolil and Seekolicks were its boatmen, as of yore. No one else was with them, and yet the painted canoe carried a treasure which they regarded with superstitious awe.

They had been sent to Portland by Doc Baker and directed to call at Ladd's bank for a message from Mr. Ladd and when it was received they were to bring it to Walla Walla. They had waited at Portland months for the message, but at last Mr. Ladd called them into the bank and handed them a straight stick cut from the shrub called Indian's-arrow, and told them to take it to Doc Baker. There was no writing or other message whatever and no markings upon the stick. The Injuns looked upon the strange message with wonder not unmixed with superstition. A plain stick of sufficient importance to be sent such a distance must be "hyas close" medicine. They showed the stick to the many tribes along the shore on their way up the stream and its fame spread along each bank of the Columbia. At the big village of Wish-ram it was taken into the council tent where a "skookum wawa" (big talk) was held, and the more fearful ones proposed its destruction, but Sapolil said it was "close" (big) medicine and if destroyed Sachem Ladd and Sachem Baker would know instantly and would call down trouble on the river tribes the same as the white man had done a few years before, whose wife and child had been slain by the cut-throats of Wish-ram while he was absent from his cabin in the mountains. Later he entered Wish-ram trembling with weakness and with the shadow of death upon his face, holding up his hands as a token that he had come in peace. The murderers were uneasy, but finally smoked the pipe of peace with the sick man, and then he arose unsteadily to his feet and cursed Wish-ram and all its people, and said that the great "Kaquilla Tyee" (Devil) would sweep the black "memaloose" (death) through all their tribes.

Then the white man frothed at the mouth with a horrible disease which had pitted his face in holes, and fell sprawling, in the council circle dead. But the "memaloose" he had foretold swept over the village and pitted their faces, and the redmen died so fast there was none to bury them.

So the bandits of Wish-ram, who lived by pillaging those who journeyed up and down the river, did not destroy the mystic stick for fear of the power of the "skookum" White Medicine Men and finally it was delivered by the Indian messengers to Doc Baker at Walla Walla.

He instantly understood the message, which meant that the sailing ship had arrived around the Horn from New York, and, swinging its tackle far out, had dropped the two locomotives on the bank of the Willamette at Portland, and that the gauge of the locomotives was the length of the stick.

Handing the stick to the Chief Engineer, who immediately started his gangs to work spiking down the loose wooden rail the whole length of the road, Doc Baker started for Portland.

The question of bringing the locomotives

and equipment up the Columbia was one of great moment not unmixed with danger. The red robbers of Wish-ram, if they permitted the locomotives to pass around the rapids at all, would exact enormous tribute, or there would be a great battle which would gradually extend to the neighboring tribes and the result might be the complete annihilation of the whites, who in the whole northwest were at that time greatly outnumbered by the Injuns.

When the barges containing the two locomotives, one hundred pairs of car wheels and the thousand plug hats arrived at the rapids of Wish-ram the wisdom of Doc Baker shone out anew. The resplendent breeches of Seekolicks, though with luster now slightly impaired by coatings of salmon scales, still continued to attract the admiring glances of Wish-ram maidens, to the instense disgust of all the other bucks who from necessity were without breeches. This general feeling was, one might say, openly and nakedly displayed without attempt at concealment. Doc Baker had studied this situation from the first and now decided to profit by working with, instead of against, human passions and desires. He called a council of the head villians of Wish-ram and with the astuteness of an oriental peddler in the ancient city of Bagdad, displayed for the first time to the astonished gaze of the assembled robbers the wonders of a dress silk hat, and with consummate cunning bargained at the price of one stove-pipe for each of the doughty warriors of Wish-ram, not only for free passage of the locomotives, but for the combined power of a thousand naked but plug-hatted villians to drag the locomotives around the rapids.

What boots it now that Seekolicks' breeches displayed the glories of a sunset (apologies to Sunset Magazine)? For influence with an Injun maiden a shiny plug hat will do more than a thousand dollars in stock of the Standard Oil Company, and Seekolicks' breeches fell behind in the mad race of changing fashions along the river.

At last the locomotives and one hundred pairs of car wheels reached Wallula, where Bill Green had built an incline running down to the water in order to bring them up to the roadway.

This he did without difficulty by hitching his great team of forty oxen to each locomotive in turn. It is safe to say that this team of oxen could pull as much as either locomotive, though not so rapidly, perhaps.

When the locomotives were at last on the main line the names "Loco Ladd" and "Loco Blue Mountain" were painted on their cab panels. Thus Doc Baker honored the two greatest objects, to him, in the world. The road was ready for service, the cars having been previously constructed entirely of wood and the car wheels brought from New York had been placed under them.

The chief engineer had conducted all these operations from the saddle of his mule. He galloped back from the leading yoke of the forty-ox team, to where Doc Baker stood near the locomotives, now on the main line, and solemnly announced to his chief that the road was ready for business. Then turning to the train dispatcher, also mounted on a long-legged mule with two big horse pistols hanging low on his hips, the chief engineer formally turned over the completed railroad from the Construction to the Operating Department in these terse terms: "Their your'n. Get to hell out o' here with 'em."

CHAPTER VII.

THE TRAIN DISPATCHER

Mindful of Mr. Ladd's suggestions, Doc Baker had selected a train dispatcher to conduct transportation on the railroad.

The train dispatcher had charge of the movement of trains, therefore he must be a man of quick action. His selection was a problem. But Doc Baker's resourcefulness was a match for all exigencies. His mind at once settled on Josh Moore as the very man for the place.

Josh could ride the worst bucking cayuse on the range, which showed his ability to handle way freight crews. A particularly bad cayuse that had defeated all others was assigned him to break. After the usual preliminaries, the horse, standing first on his head and then on his hind feet rolled over, but when the cayuse was on his back Josh was still astride the animal's belly, and when the cayuse arose to all fours again, he found the rider still on his back. Then as a last resort the cayuse took the bit and bolted for the low limb of a spreading oak tree to scrape Josh off, but the latter merely rose to his feet on the animal's back, vaulted over the limb and landed astride of the cayuse on the other side. The cayuse was vanquished, but Josh had lost his boots.

Many stories are told of Josh's familiarity with the Henry rifle. It is said that an Injun once stole his horse and outfit and before Josh could get to his gun, galloped out of sight around the south side of a hill. Without waiting an instant Josh swung the gun to his shoulder and sighting a rock wall on a detached peak to the north of the hill, fired. The bullet caromed on the rock wall and passing behind the hill brought down the fleeing Injun. This showed keen ability to make good meeting points without loss of time to either of the moving objects.

The ability to make meeting points and to withstand the bucking of the local freight crews being the principal qualifications of a train dispatcher as laid down by the philosophy of Pat Prunty, Josh Moore was inducted into the office. The chief engineer and train dispatcher comprised all the officers of the road. The train dispatcher hired a discharged fireman and a deckhand from a river boat at Portland and they were put in charge of the locomotives as engineers at salaries of $50.00 per month each. Then he hired two cowboys off the range for firemen at $75.00 each, reasoning that the firemens' work was harder than the engineers'. Telegraph systems were not to be thought of, but Josh Moore was mounted on a swift mule and equipped with two horse pistols (which he said had been raised from Colt's) and by a code of signals comprising pistol shots he galloped from one train to the other and gave his orders in such a manner that the crews had no difficulty in getting them through their heads without back talk which train dispatchers meet with nowadays.

Doubtless many a train dispatcher, housed at a big terminal, who may read this account of primitive railroading will long for the simple but effective methods of Josh Moore.

THE TRAIN DISPATCHER

But the most intensely practical side of the train dispatcher was perhaps best illustrated in his conception of the locomotive pilots sometimes called "cowcatchers." When the locomotives first arrived at Wallula the train dispatcher, taking Pat Prunty the source of all railroad wisdom, along with him, proceeded to look them over. He inquired of Prunty the purpose of the "V" shaped combination of slats on the front ends of the locomotives. Prunty explained that these were called "cowcatchers" and were to clear the track of cattle. The train dispatcher remarked that the bunch of corset staves might be serviceable for catching cows in the City of New York, but in the great west cows were harder to catch and more dangerous when caught. His authority in reality being as absolute as the country operator thinks the authority of the average dispatcher is today, he ordered the pilots ripped off the two locomotives and low platforms built in their stead. On each of these platforms he stationed one of his best hunting dogs which he quickly trained, when cattle on the tracks were approached, to leap to the ground and drive them away. The dogs at once grasped the responsibility of their import-

THE COWCATCHER

ant railroad positions and thirty minutes before departure of each train from their respective terminals at Walla Walla and Wallula, without the service of the caller, they took their positions on their locomotive platforms and, like the great figure heads on the ship prows of the conquering Vikings, they piloted the trains across the Walla Walla valley faithful to their duties as "cowcatchers" in fact as well as in name.

The Rawhide Railroad, though operating in a cattle country, under the wise direction of Bill Green and Josh Moore paid fewer claims for cattle killed according to its size than any other railroad in the world.

Nor did the two "cowcatchers," "Ponto" and "Thor" ever "bark" on account of their over-time being short on payday. They were watchful of other things besides six o'clock and the pay car.

After taking formal charge of the road at Wallula, Josh Moore ordered the engines fired up with wood and the run made to Walla Walla. After the fires had been burning in the boxes for a time something let go on one of the engines with such a terrific crash that the assembled cowboys galloped frantically across the prairie to a place of safety and the thousand naked plug-hatted pirates from Wish-ram, thinking that the end had come, plunged headlong over the bank and into the Columbia's seething depths. Even the chief engineer and train dispatcher controlled themselves with difficulty and tried to look as if they had a life-long familiarity with the blowing off of safety valves.

In time the locomotives on wooden rails reached Walla Walla and were received there with the same speeches that are always made under such circumstances.

CHAPTER VIII.

DESTRUCTION OF THE RAILROAD

Soon it was found that the gnawing movements of the tread and flanges of the locomotive drivers quickly wore off the tops and edges of the wooden rails making it necessary constantly to renew them.

The pioneer of the Pacific coast has one favorite "metal" on which he relies to surmount all difficulties—the renowned rawhide. He who understands it can accomplish wonders with it. But its antics are strange to those from eastern lands, unfamiliar with its peculiar properties.

The pioneers delight to tell of the tender-foot who did not know how rawhide would

stretch when wet and contract when dry. He hitched up his team with rawhide harness in a rain storm, and attached a drag chain to a log, intending to pull it to his cabin for fuel. Driving the team to the cabin, he looked back and saw that the log had not moved, the rain causing the rawhile harness to stretch all the way to the house. Disgusted, he unharnessed the horses and threw the harness over a stump. The sun came out, and contracting the harness, pulled the log up to the house.

Possessed of enormous qualities of this durable material, Doc Baker directed that the wooden rails be "plated" with rawhide from

Walla Walla to Wallula. It hardened in the summer sun and made the roadway practically indestructible.

In the rainy season the rawhide became soft and the road could not be operated, but there was no occasion to operate it in the winter time for the reason that there was no traffic, and when the snow melted in the spring, the sun blazing out over the valley quickly put the rawhide railroad in good condition and ready for train service.

Finally there came a winter of terrible severity on the Pacific coast which was long spoken of as the "hard winter."

In the empire of Walla Walla it did untold damage. The snow fell very deep throughout the land. With the first rains and snows the rawhide railroad ceased operation for the winter, according to its usual custom, as the rawhide had become soft as mush.

Provisions became scarce. Great hardships and suffering were experienced. Cattle raisers were obliged to begin feeding their stock earlier than usual and soon the feed ran short. In desperation they turned the cattle out on the range, which was covered with deep snow. Blizzards swept over the prairie lands and many of the cattle froze to death standing erect, a gruesome sight.

The deer in the Blue Mountains were starved and frozen and the wolves from the fastnesses of the distant Rockies on the east and from ice-bound Canada on the north swept over the country devouring the carcasses of the frozen deer and after these were all gone, forced on by famishing hunger, and growing bolder as the winter became more and more severe, they crept out over the great valley of Walla Walla in search of food.

Driven at last in desperation, to sustain their lives, the red-throated, ravening monsters, running in great packs, crowded on and on to the very edge of the village of Walla Walla, searching for carcasses of frozen cattle which they pawed out of the snow and quickly devoured.

The beleagured village now felt that it was only a question of days, perhaps hours, if the

storm did not break, when they would have to fight the oncoming horde of famished fiends to preserve their very lives. And everyone was prepared for the final conflict.

One night, late in midwinter, the blizzard was roaring and howling across the prairie and snow was falling in long slanting sheets, when a tremendous disturbance was made at the door of Doc Baker's home.

Grabbing up a loaded pistol, the doctor ran to the door, fearing the last stand against the wolves was at hand. Opening the door cautiously, he saw outside the two faithful Injuns, Sapolil and Seekolicks, seeking admission. They hurled their shivering bodies through the doorway and began in a mixture of English and Chinook, a wild effort to communicate some disastrous intelligence to their friend, Doc Baker.

Their excitement was so great that the only word the doctor could catch in the first rush of their attempt to talk, was "wolves."

Without waiting for more, the doctor called to all the men of the household to arm themselves quickly and prepare for a fight against the coming onslaught of the wolves. Then turning to his sideboard he poured a good big drink of strong whiskey for each of the Injuns, now trembling with cold and excitement. This disposed of, he pushed them down by the roaring fire-place and forced them to deliver their message slowly and in a manner that could be understood.

In broken English, interwoven with Chinook, Sapolil finally succeeded in disclosing the terrible information, which ran as follows:

"Railroad—him gonum hell. Damn wolves "digum out—eatum all up—Wallula to Walla "Walla."

THE END.

TAILENDUM

Now read the last paragraph of the Headendum.

SHOREY
Publications Catalog

1. Glover, S.L. ORIGIN AND OCCURENCE OF GEM STONES IN WASHINGTON. 1949 — 1.00
2. Mooney, Jas. Ghost Dance Religion: SMOHALLA AND HIS DOCTRINE. 1896 — 1.50
3. Mooney. Ghost Dance Religion: SHAKERS OF PUGET SOUND. 1896 — 1.50
5. DICTIONARY OF CHINOOK JARGON. nd — 2.00
6. ALASKA RAILROAD TIME TABLES. 1922 — .50
7. Wells, E.H. UP AND DOWN THE YUKON. 1900 — 1.50
8. Williams, J.G. REPORT OF ATTORNEY GENERAL, Territory of Alaska, 1949-51. — 1.50
9. Gruening, Ernest. MESSAGE OF THE GOVERNOR OF ALASKA, 1946. — 2.00
10. Gruening. THIRD MESSAGE TO THE PEOPLE OF ALASKA, 1946. — 1.50
11. Kohlstedt, E.D. A GLIMPSE OF ALASKA. 1930 — 1.00
12. Gruening. MESSAGE OF THE GOVERNOR OF ALASKA, 1945. — 2.50
13. Leehey, M.D. PUBLIC LAND POLICY OF THE U.S. IN ALASKA. 1912 — 1.50
14. NOME TELEPHONE DIRECTORY. 1905 — 3.00
15. ESTABLISHMENT OF MT. MCKINLEY NATIONAL PARK. 1916 — 1.50
16. Hooper, Capt. C.L. CRUISE OF THE U.S. REVENUE STEAMER CORWIN IN ARCTIC
    OCEAN, November 1, 1880. — 7.50
17. Gruening. MESSAGE TO THE PEOPLE OF ALASKA. 1945 — 2.00
18. Gruening. MESSAGES OF THE GOVERNOR OF ALASKA. 1949 — 2.50
19. Davis, Geo. T. METLAKAHTLA. 1904 — 3.50
20. WORK OF THE BUREAU OF EDUCATION FOR NATIVES OF ALASKA. 1918 — 5.00
21. MacDowell, L.W. ALASKA INDIAN BASKETRY. — 1.00
22. Eells, Rev. Myron. THE TWANA, CHEMAKUM & KLALLAM INDIANS OF WASHINGTON
    TERRITORY. 1887 — 4.00
23. Grinnell, Joseph. GOLD HUNTING IN ALASKA. — 4.00
24. Swan, James G. INDIANS OF CAPE FLATTERY. — 7.50
25. CUSTER'S LAST BATTLE. 1892 — 2.00
26. Gruening, Sen. INDEPENDENCE DAY ADDRESS. 1959 — 1.75
27. Cadell, H.M. THE KLONDIKE AND YUKON GOLDFIELD IN 1913. 1914 — 2.50
28. Shiels, Archie W. EARLY VOYAGES OF THE PACIFIC. 1930 — 3.00
29. Fickett, E.D. METEOROLOGY. From Explorations in Alaska. 1900
30. Richardson, W.P. & others. YUKON RIVER EXPLORING EXPEDITION. Expl. in Alaska.
    1900 — 2.00
31. Ray, P.H., W.P. Richardson. RELIEF OF THE DESTITUTE IN THE GOLDFIELDS.
    1900 — 1.75
32. Shiels, Archie W. LITTLE JOURNEYS INTO THE HISTORY OF RUSSIAN AMERICA AND
    PURCHASE OF ALASKA. 1949 — 7.50
33. Shiels. STORY OF TWO DREAMS. 1957 — 4.00
34. Swan, J.G. HAIDAH INDIANS OF QUEEN CHARLOTTE'S ISLAND, B.C. 1874 — 5.00
35. Butler, Gen. B.V. & the Marquis of Lorne. THE BERING SEA CONTROVERSY.
    1892 — 1.50
36. Crawford, Lewis F. THE MEDORA-DEADWOOD STAGE LINE. 1925 — 1.50
37. Anderson, Eskil. ASBESTOS AND JADE OCCURENCES IN KOBUK RIVER REGION,
    Alaska. 1945 — 2.00
38. Stewart, B.D. PROSPECTING IN ALASKA. 1949 — 1.50
39. Geoghegan, Richard H. THE ALEUT LANGUAGE. — 5.00
40. SEATTLE'S FIRST BUSINESS DIRECTORY. 1876 — 7.50
41. THE WASHBURN YELLOWSTONE EXPEDITION. 1871 — 1.25
42. Subreports from EXPLORATIONS IN ALASKA. 7 reports: The Tanana, Chickaloon,
    Sushitna, etc. 1900 — 2.00
43. Glenn, Capt. E.F. TANANA RIVER EXPLORING EXPEDITION. 1900 — 2.50
44. Glenn. COOK'S INLET EXPLORING EXPEDITION. 1900 — 1.75
45. WILKESON'S NOTES ON PUGET SOUND (1870?) — 2.50
46. (Perry). JOURNAL OF A VOYAGE TO THE ARCTIC REGIONS IN H.M.S. ALEXANDER,
    1818. (1819?) — 6.00
47. BIENNIAL MESSAGE OF WM. M. BUNN, Governor of Idaho. 1884 — 2.00
48. MACKENZIE'S ROCK. Exploration of Sir Alexander Mackenzie. 1905 — 2.50
49. Williams, L.R. OUR PACIFIC COUNTY (Wash) — 5.00
50. AARON LADNER LINDSLEY..Founder of Alaska Missions. — 1.00
51. Evans, Elwood. PUGET SOUND: Its Past, Present and Future. 1869 — 2.50
52. Campbell, Robt. TWO JOURNALS, 1808-1853. — 15.00
53. Bernhardi, Madame Charlotte. MEMOIR OF THE CELEBRATED ADM. JOHN de
    KRUSENSTERN. 1856 — 5.00
54. McWhorter, Lucullus V. CRIME AGAINST THE YAKIMAS. 1931 — 4.50
55. Lupton, Chas T. OIL AND GAS IN THE OLYMPIC PENINSULA. 1913 — 4.00
56. Seward, Wm. H. THE ADMISSION OF KANSAS. A Speech. 1860 — 1.50
57. Stevens, Issac I. PROCLAMATION OF MARTIAL LAW. 1856 — .50
58. THE GLACIER - Tlinkit Training Academy, Vol. II. 1887 — .75
59. Hills, Rev. E.P. REV. AARON L. LINDSLEY. — .50
60. SWANTON'S HANDBOOK OF NORTH AMERICAN INDIANS, Pt. C: Indians of Alaska &
    Canada. 1952 — 5.00
61. Ward, D.B. ACROSS THE PLAINS IN 1853. 1911 — 3.50
62. MacDowell, Lloyd W. ALASKA TOTEM POLES. — 1.25
63. MacDowell. A TRIP TO WONDERFUL ALASKA. — 2.00
64. MacDowell. ALASKA GLACIERS & ICE FIELDS. — 1.25
65. Shaw, Geo. C. THE CHINOOK JARGON AND HOW TO USE IT. 1909 — 4.00

134b. Hodge. *MINING IN CENTRAL & EASTERN WASHINGTON.* Ext. from #134 — 10.00
134c. Hodge. *MINING IN SOUTHERN BRITISH COLUMBIA.* Ext. from #134 — 10.00
135. Stallard, Bruce. *ARCHEOLOGY IN WASHINGTON.* 1958 — 3.00
136. Lockley, Fred. *ALASKA'S FIRST FREE MAIL DELIVERY IN 1900.* — 1.25
137. Strange. *JAMES STRANGE'S JOURNAL AND NARRATIVE OF THE COMMERCIAL EXPEDITION FROM BOMBAY TO THE NORTHWEST COAST OF AMERICA.* 1928 — 5.00
138. Hathaway, Ella C. *BATTLE OF THE BIG HOLE.* — 2.00
139. Haller, Granville. *SAN JUAN & SECESSION.* — 1.50
140. *THE KLONDIKE NEWS.* Vol. 1 #1, Dawson Newspaper. 1898 (Alaska's rarest newspaper) — 10.00
141. *JOURNAL OF MEDOREM CRAWFORD.* 1897 — 2.00
142. *OCOSTA!* The Ocean Terminus of the Northern Pacific R.R. and Coast City of Washington. — 2.50
143. Sutherland, T.A. *HOWARD'S CAMPAIGN AGAINST THE NEZ PERCE INDIANS, 1877.* 1878 — 3.50
144. Matthews, Mathew. *THE CATLIN COLLECTION OF INDIAN PAINTINGS.* 1890 — 3.00
145. Lockley, Fred. *TO OREGON BY OX TEAM IN '47.* — 1.25
146. Lockley. *VIGILANTE DAYS IN VIRGINIA CITY.* — 1.50
147. Judson, Katherine. *MYTHS AND LEGENDS OF THE PACIFIC NORTHWEST.* 1910 — 7.50
148. Whiting, Dr. F.B. *GRIT, GRIEF AND GOLD.* — 10.00
149. Amundsen, Capt. Roald. *TO THE NORTH MAGNETIC POLE AND THROUGH THE NORTHWEST PASSAGE.* — 3.00
150. Butte Businessmen's Assn. *BUTTE, MONTANA.* — 2.00
151. Immigration Aid Society of Washington Terr. *NORTHWESTERN WASHINGTON.* 1880 — 3.50
152. Denig, Edwin T. *INDIAN TRIBES OF THE UPPER MISSOURI.* 1930 — 10.00
153. Buckley, Rev. J.M. *TWO WEEKS IN THE YOSEMITE AND VICINITY.* 1888 — 2.50
154. *SPEECH OF THE HON. R.C. WINTHROP OF MASS. ON THE PRESIDENT'S MESSAGE* (on admission of California) 1850 — 2.00
155. Marshall, Martha. *A PRONOUNCING DICTIONARY OF CALIFORNIA NAMES IN ENGLISH AND SPANISH.* — 2.50
156. Mercer, A.S. *BIG HORN COUNTY, WYOMING.* — 7.50
157. Moorehead, Warren K. *PREHISTORIC RELICS.* — 7.50
158. Merrill, Geo. P. *NOTES ON THE GEOLOGY AND NATURAL HISTORY OF THE PENINSULA OF LOWER CALIFORNIA.* 1895 — 2.00
159. Georgeson, C.C. *REINDEER & CARIBOU.* 1904 — 1.50
160. Hewett, Edgar L. *A GENERAL VIEW OF THE ARCHEOLOGY OF THE PUEBLO REGION.* 1904 — 2.00
161. Bennett, Wm. P. *THE FIRST BABY IN CAMP.* — 3.50
162. Coffman, Noah B. *OLD LEWIS COUNTY, Oregon Territory.* 1926 — 3.50
163. Bebbe, Mrs. Iola. *THE TRUE LIFE STORY OF SWIFTWATER BILL GATES.* 1908 — 7.50
164. Costello. *THE SIWASH - THEIR LIFE, LEGENDS AND TALES.* 1895 — 10.00
165. Murie, Olaus J. *ALASKA-YUKON CARIBOU.* — 10.00
166. Meeker, Ezra. *STORY OF THE LOST TRAIL TO OREGON, NO. 2.* 1916 — 2.50
167. Hanna, Rev. J.A. *DR. WHITMAN AND HIS RIDE TO SAVE OREGON.* 1903 — 1.25
168. Hadwen, Seymore & Laurence J. Palmer. *REINDEER IN ALASKA.* 1922 — 5.00
169. Geer, T.T. *THE ROMANCE OF ASTORIA.* 1911 — 1.75
170. Williams, Lewis. *CHINOOK BY THE SEA.* — 7.50
171. *SAN FERNANDO VALLEY.* 1938 — 2.00
172. *PASADENA.* 1938 — 2.00
173. Ingalls, Maj. J.W. *HISTORY OF WASHOE COUNTY, NEVADA.* 1913 — 5.00
174. Reid, J.T. & J.R. Hunter. *HUMBOLT COUNTY.* 1913 — 4.50
175. Aston. *ESMERALDA COUNTY.* 1913 — 4.50
176. London, Jack. *THE GOLD HUNTERS OF THE NORTH.* Ext., 1903. — 1.25
177. Wartman-Arland, Flora E. *THE STORY OF MONTESANO.* 1933 — 4.00
178. London. *THE ECONOMICS OF THE KLONDIKE.* — 1.50
179. Bishop, Robert Sr. *LAND IN THE SKY TOTEM.* — 1.50
180. Webb, John S. & Ed S. Curtis. *THE RIVER TRIP TO THE KLONDIKE AND THE RUSH TO THE KLONDIKE OVER THE MOUNTAIN PASS.* 1898 — 2.50
181. Librn. of Bellingham Public Libr. *HISTORY OF BELLINGHAM.* 1926 — 6.00
182. *VOYAGE OF ALEXANDER MACKENZIE.* — 2.50
183. Chaplin, Ralph. *CENTRALIA CONSPIRACY.* — 4.50
184. Haswell, Robert. *ROBERT HASWELL'S JOURNALS.* 1788-89. — 4.00
185. Minto, John. *RHYME OF EARLY LIFE IN OREGON.* (1915?) — 4.00
186. Collins, Henry B., A.H. Clarke & E.H. Walker. *THE ALEUTIAN ISLANDS: Their People & Natural History.* 1945 — 7.50
187. Simpson, Brevet Brig. Gen. J.H. *CORONADO'S MARCH IN SEARCH OF THE "SEVEN CITIES OF CIBOLA."* 1871 — 2.50
188. Riddle, Geo. W. *EARLY DAYS IN OREGON.* — 5.00
189. *VILHJALMUR STEFANSON.* 1925 — 2.50
190. Lockley, Fred. *ACROSS THE PLAINS BY PRAIRIE SCHOONER.* — 1.50
191. MacArthur, Walter. *LAST DAYS OF SAIL ON THE WEST COAST.* 1929 — 7.50
192. Stuck, Hudson. *THE ALASKAN MISSIONS OF THE EPISCOPAL CHURCH.* 1920 — 10.00
193. Steffa, Don. *TALES OF NOTED FRONTIER CHARACTERS, SOAPY SMITH.* 1908 — 1.75
194. Meeker, E. *WASHINGTON TERRITORY* 1870 — 3.00
195. Denny, Arthur A. *PIONEER DAYS ON PUGET SOUND.* 1888 — 5.00
196. Rowan, James. *THE I.W.W. IN THE LUMBER INDUSTRY.* — 4.00
199. Sayre, J. Willis. *THE EARLY WATERFRONT OF SEATTLE, 1937.* — 2.50

204.	Pelly, T.M. DR. MINOR - A SKETCH OF HIS BACKGROUND AND LIFE. 1933	7.50
209.	Flandrau, Grace. FRONTIER DAYS ALONG THE UPPER MISSOURI.	3.00
210.	Flandrau. THE LEWIS AND CLARK EXPEDITION.	5.00
211.	Flandrau. A GLANCE AT THE LEWIS AND CLARK EXPEDITION.	3.00
213.	Flandrau. THE VERENDRYE OVERLAND QUEST OF THE PACIFIC.	3.50
216.	Harper, Frank B. FORT UNION AND ITS NEIGHBORS ON THE UPPER MISSOURI.	2.50
220.	Burdick, Usher L. MARQUIS de MORES AT WAR IN THE BADLANDS. 1929	2.50
227.	General Strike Committee. THE SEATTLE GENERAL STRIKE. 1919	5.00
231.	Sayre, J.W. THE ROMANCE OF SECOND AVENUE.	1.50
235.	DEDICATION AND OPENING OF THE NEW CASCADE TUNNEL. 1929	2.00
239.	Van Olinda, O.S. HISTORY OF VASHON - MAURY ISLAND. 1935	6.00
241.	Hanford, C.H. SAN JUAN DISPUTE. 1900	2.00
246.	Walgamott, C.S. REMINISCENCES OF EARLY DAYS. 1926	7.50
250.	Wardner, Jim. JIM WARDNER, OF WARDNER IDAHO. 1900	8.00
251.	Brown, Col. W.C. THE SHEEPEATER CAMPAIGN, Idaho - 1879. 1926	2.50
259.	Hornaday, Wm. T. EXTERMINATION OF THE AMERICAN BISON. 1887?	10.00
264.	Slauson, Morda C. ONE HUNDRED YEARS ON THE CEDAR.	10.00
265.	Jones, S.C. & M.F. Casady. FROM CABIN TO CUPOLA. County Courthouses in Washington.	10.00
267.	Andrews, Clarence L. WRANGELL AND THE GOLD OF THE CASSIAR. 1937	3.50
268.	Andrews, Clarence L. THE PIONEERS AND THE NUGGETS OF VERSE. 1937	3.00
280.	PORT TOWNSEND. 1890	5.00
281.	Gilbert, Kenneth. ALASKAN POKER STORIES. 1958	2.50
282.	Moore, James Bernard. SKAGWAY IN DAYS PRIMEVAL.	4.00
283.	Chase, Cora G. UNTO THE LEAST - A Biographic Sketch of Mother Ryther. 1972	6.00
284.	Blankenship, Geo. E. EARLY HISTORY OF THURSTON COUNTY. 1914	20.00
285.	Fish, Harriet U. PAST AT PRESENT In Issaquah, Wn. 1967	12.50
286.	Allen, Edward W. THE ROLLICKING PACIFIC; A Selection of Poems. 1972	3.00
287.	Allen. DANCING TALES AND OTHER FISHY JINGLES. 1951	4.00
289.	Chin, Doug & Art. UPHILL - The Settlement & Diffusion of the Chinese in Seattle.	6.00
292.	Harpham, Josephine E. DOORWAYS INTO HISTORY - Early Houses & Public Buildings of Oregon.	5.00
SJU 1.	Farlow, Dr. W.G. SOME EDIBLE AND POISONOUS FUNGI. 1897	2.50
SJU 2.	Gurdji, V. ORIENTAL RUG WEAVING. 1901	5.00
SJU 3.	D'Avenes, E., Prisse & Dr. J.C. Ewart. EGYPTIAN AND ARABIAN HORSES AND ORIGIN OF HORSES AND PONIES. 1904	2.50
SJU 4.	Freshfield, Douglas W. ON MOUNTAINS AND MANKIND. 1904	1.50
SJU 5.	Davenport, Cyril. CAMEOS. 1904	1.50
SJU 6.	Maire, Albert. MATERIALS USED TO WRITE UPON BEFORE THE INVENTION OF PRINTING.	1.50
SJU 7.	Liberty, Arthur L. PEWTER AND THE REVIVAL OF ITS USE. 1904	1.50
SJU 8.	Hammell, Wm. PINE NEEDLE BASKETRY.	1.50
SJU 9.	Frey, Clark, Vietch. HOME TANNING. 1936	1.50
SJU 10.	Browning, Frank. STEAM PLANT ERRORS.	2.00
SJU 18.	Burdick, Arthur J. THE PROSPECTOR'S MANUAL. 1905	7.50
SJU 19.	WOODS DUAL POWER. (1902?)	1.50
SJU 20.	Hayward, Charles B. DIRIGIBLE BALLOONS. 1921	5.00
SJU 21.	Osborn, Henry F. THE ELEPHANTS AND MASTEDONS ARRIVE IN AMERICA.	1.50
SJU 22.	Todd, Mattie Phipps. HAND LOOM WEAVING. 1902	7.00
SJU 23.	Wilbur, C. Martin. HISTORY OF THE CROSSBOW. 1936	1.50
SJU 24.	Alexander, A.S. HORSE SECRETS. 1913	2.50
SJU 26.	Clute, Willard Nelson. THE FERN - COLLECTOR'S GUIDE. 1901	3.00
SJU 27.	Meeker, E. HOP CULTURE IN THE U.S. 1883	10.00
SJU 28.	Austin-Walker Sales Co. APACHE BEADWORK - Instructions and Designs	2.50
SJU 29.	Holmstrom, J.G. SCIENTIFIC HORSE, MULE & OX SHOEING. 1902	4.00
SJU 30.	Fickes, Clyde P. & W. Ellis Groben. BUILDING WITH LOGS. 1945	2.50
SJI 1.	Krause, F. SLING CONTRIVANCES. 1904	2.00
SJI 2.	Murdoch, John. A STUDY OF THE ESKIMO BOWS IN THE U.S. NATIONAL MUSEUM. 1884	1.50
SJI 3.	Mason, Otis T. THROWING STICKS IN THE NATIONAL MUSEUM. 1884	2.50
SJI 4.	CHIEF JOSEPH'S OWN STORY. 1879	2.50
SJI 5.	Mason, Otis. BASKET WORK OF THE ABORIGINES. 1884	5.00
SJI 6.	Llwd, Rev. Dr. J.P.D. THE MESSAGE OF AN INDIAN RELIC: Seattle's Totem Pole.	2.00
SJI 7.	Mason, O. TRAPS OF THE AMERICAN INDIAN.	1.25
SJI 8.	Meeker, Louis L. OGALALA GAMES. 1901	1.50
SJI 9.	Collins, Henry B. PREHISTORIC ART OF THE ALASKAN ESKIMO. 1929	3.50
SJI 10.	Eells, Rev. M. JUSTICE TO THE INDIAN.	1.00
SJI 11.	Willoughby, C. INDIANS OF THE QUINAIELT AGENCY, Washington Territory. 1886	1.50
SJI 12.	Leon & Holmes. STUDIES ON THE ARCHAEOLOGY OF MICHOACAN MEXICO...1886	2.00
SJI 13.	Beckwith, Paul. NOTES ON CUSTOMS OF THE DAKOTAHS. 1886	1.25
SJI 14.	Eells, Rev. M. THE STONE AGE. 1886	1.50
SJI 15.	Allen, Lt. Henry T. ATNATANAS NATIVES OF COPPER RIVER, ALASKA. 1886	1.00
SJI 16.	Yates, Dr. L.G. CHARM STONES. 1886	1.50

SJI 20. Gibbs, Geo., Dr. Wm. F. Tolmie, & Father G. Mengarini. *TRIBES OF WESTERN WASHINGTON AND NORTHWESTERN OREGON.*   20.00

SJI 21. Gibbs, Geo., & others. *COMPARATIVE VOCABULARIES OF THE TRIBES OF WESTERN WASHINGTON AND NORTHWESTERN OREGON. part of SJI #20.*   5.00

SJI 22. Gibbs, Geo. *A DICTIONARY OF THE NISQUALLY INDIAN LANGUAGE. part of SJI #20.*   10.00

SJI 23. Boas, Franz. *INTRODUCTION TO HANDBOOK OF AMERICAN INDIAN LANGUAGES. Ext. 1911*   5.00

SJI 24. Swanton, John R. *THE TLINGIT INDIAN LANGUAGE. From Hndbk of American Indian Language.*   3.00

SJI 25. Swanton. *THE HAIDA INDIAN LANGUAGE.*   5.00

SJI 26. Boas. *THE TSIMSHIAN INDIAN LANGUAGE.*   8.00

SJI 27. Boas. *THE KWAKIUTL INDIAN LANGUAGE.*   7.50

SJI 28. Boas. *THE CHINOOK INDIAN LANGUAGE.*   5.00

SJI 29. Boas & Swanton. *THE SIOUAN, DAKOTA INDIAN LANGUAGE.*   6.00

SJI 30. Talbitzer, Wm. *THE ESKIMO LANGUAGE.*   6.50

SJI 31. Ewers, John C. *EARLY WHITE INFLUENCE UPON PLAINS INDIAN PAINTING. 1957*   2.00

SJI 32. Fenton, Wm. N. *CONTRACTS BETWEEN IROQUOIS HERBALISM AND COLONIAL MEDICINE. 1941*   2.00

SJI 38. Remington, Fred. *ARTIST WANDERINGS AMONG THE CHEYENNES. 1889*   1.50

SJI 41. Bagley, Clarence. *INDIAN MYTHS OF THE NORTHWEST. 1930*   8.50

SJI 43. Mason, O. *ABORIGINAL SKIN DRESSING.*   5.00

SJI 46. Thorne, J. Frederic. *IN THE TIME THAT WAS. 1909*   2.50

SJI 49. DeSmet, Rev. P.J. *NEW INDIAN SKETCHES.*   8.50

SJI 51. Mason, O. *MAN'S KNIFE AMONG THE NORTH AMERICAN INDIANS. 1899*   2.00

SJI 53. Holmes, William H. *POTTERY OF THE ANCIENT PUEBLOS. 1886*   6.00

SJI 55. Dorsey, James O. *A STUDY OF SIOUAN CULTS. 1894*   10.00

SJI 57. Mason, O. *POINTED BARK CANOES OF THE KUTENAI AND AMUR. 1901*   2.00

SJI 58. Mason, O. *ABORIGINAL AMERICAN HARPOONS. 1902*   7.50

SJI 59. Hough, Walter. *THE LAMP OF THE ESKIMO. 1898*   5.00

SJI 61. Drucker, Philip. *ARCHAEOLOGICAL SURVEY ON THE NORTHERN NORTHWEST COAST. 1943*   7.00

SJI 62. *INDIANS IN WASHINGTON.*   3.00

SJI 64. Steward, Julian H. *PETROGLYPHS OF THE U.S. Ext. 1936*   2.00

SJI 67. Shallcross, V.W. *AMERICAN LANGUAGE IN THE KIRILLIC ALPHABET.*   5.00

SJI 68. Fletcher, Alice C. *HOME LIFE AMONG THE INDIANS. 1897*   1.50

SJI 70. Teit, James & Franz Boas. *SALISHAN TRIBES OF THE WESTERN PLATEAUS. 1930*   15.00

SJI 70A Teit & Boas. *COEUR D'ALENE INDIANS. Ext from B.A.E. #45. 1930*   9.00

SJI 70B Teit & Boas. *THE OKANAGAN INDIANS. Ext from B.A.E. #45. 1930*   7.50

SJI 70C Teit & Boas. *THE FLATHEAD GROUP. Ext from B.A.E. #45. 1930*   7.50

SJI 75. Mason, Otis Tufton. *A PRIMITIVE FRAME FOR WEAVING NARROW FABRICS. 1901*   2.50

SJI 76. Millikin, Linna Loehr. *PINE NEEDLE BASKETRY. 1920*   3.00

SJI 77. *PURPLE DYEING - Ancient and Modern. 1840's*   1.50

SJI 78. Austin-Walker Sales Co. *APACHE BEADWORK - Instructions & Designs.*   2.50

NOTE TO STUDENTS AND COLLECTORS

Many scarce items turn up in antiquarian book stores only once. And while such works are in great demand, the high prices usually commanded by the older, scarcer items put them beyond the reach of the average student and the small collector. To meet this need we are bringing back into print a diversity of Pacific Northwest and Alaskan historical material which we are selling at moderate prices. In their original form these bring prices ranging from $3.00 to $100.00; some even higher.

We limit most reproductions from 25 to 100 copies and reprint as the demand warrants. The books have heavy paper covers. They show both original and reprinting dates. Regular library and dealer discounts granted. For detailed descriptions of these titles send for Shorey's Catalog of Publications #3. It also lists future Shorey Publications.

WILFRED AND OLBERT's
EPIC PREHISTORIC ADVENTURE

Written and illustrated by *Lomp*

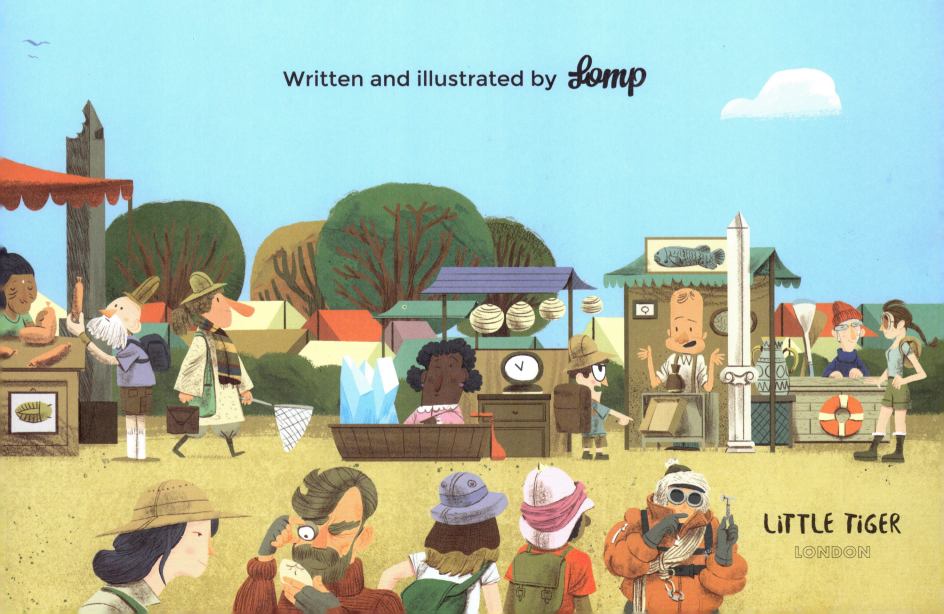

LITTLE TIGER
LONDON

One fine afternoon, Wilfred Wiseman and Olbert Oddbottom, two famous animal explorers, are out shopping when Olbert makes an exciting discovery . . .

Quick as a flash, Ollie pulls Will into the time portal!

Wilfred and Olbert dive into the portal.
Will they get back home?

DANG! That didn't work. Will and Ollie find themselves in the age of the first dinosaurs. It's the Triassic period, over 200 million years ago.

BRRRR! Will and Ollie follow the monkey through the portal into an ice age in the Quaternary period. Will they get their time machine back?

. . . arrive back home, just in time for tea! HOORAY!

At last, Wilfred and Olbert can relax.

10

One animal doesn't belong in this book. Can you spot it?

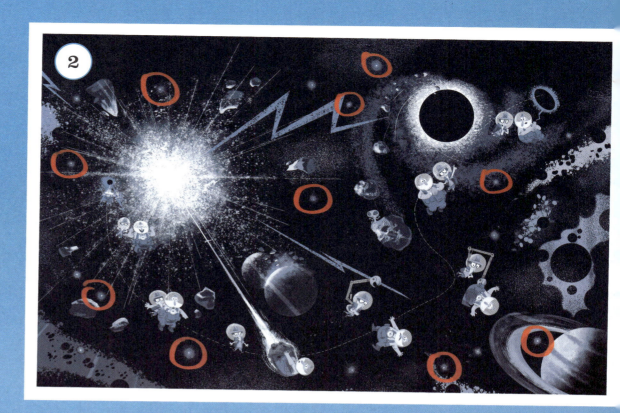

Here are the solutions to the puzzles. Did you solve them all?

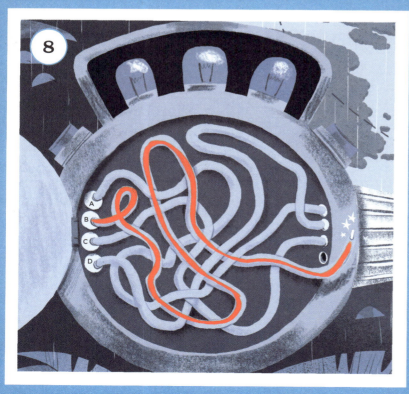